HUNGARIAN COOKING

Ruth Bauder Kershner

WEATHERVANE
BOOKS

contents

introduction

In the ninth century A.D. the nomadic Magyars swept down from the Russian steppes and settled around the Danube. They brought with them their "bogracs," iron kettles, and cooked the first aromatic gulyas over their open fires. Through the centuries the land along the Danube has been conquered by many other nations. The Hungarian people took the best each conqueror had to offer and incorporated it into their cuisine. Today, Hungary is still an agricultural nation. Her people are known throughout Central Europe for the delicious and unique cuisine that has evolved through the centuries and for their wonderful hospitality.

Hungary has historically been the Central European crossroads of East and West. Genghis Khan and his Mongol horde occupied the land around A.D. 1241. They were followed by the Turks, who occupied Hungary during the sixteenth and seventeenth centuries. The occupation was stern, and the people remained poor. During this period, gypsy caravans rolled into Hungary as they did through much of Europe during that time. They brought with them an oriental influence and their bright and lively music.

The harsh Turkish occupation was followed by a more civilized but not more pleasant occupation by the Hapsburgs. They brought with them the court cuisine of France and Austria with its fine pastries and elegant sauces. Marriage can also have been said to play an important part in the development of Hungarian cooking. During the Middle Ages, King Matthias I of Hungary married Princess Beatrice of Italy. Princess Beatrice brought with her Italian cooks and cookbooks of the period to prepare food for the court. She introduced light dumplings, pasta, and rich pastries to the cuisine. These remain today in a very refined form. Hungary has also been influenced by her neighbors. For example, the popular Hungarian dish lecsó is said to have originated in Serbia.

Today Hungary is basically an agricultural nation relying on home-grown foodstuffs and heavily dependent on the seasons. The food is hearty, and Hungary enjoys one of the highest per capita caloric consumptions in Europe. Pork is the most popular meat, followed by beef and milk-fed veal. Lamb is eaten at Easter time and is eaten frequently in sheepherding districts. Hungarian bacon and sausages are world-renowned, and many types are made. Bacon, roasted over an open fire, sprinkled with paprika and eaten with plenty of crusty bread and onions is a country favorite. Open-air spit roasting is still a favorite cooking method frequently used in the countryside. Soups and stews remain the backbone of the diet. Milk, butter, cheese and sour cream are used lavishly in cooking, adding richness to many simple dishes.

Poultry is a Hungarian favorite. In the summer flocks of geese and chickens are carefully tended and fattened for future consumption. Goose liver is especially prized and is unusually large in size. It is said to rival French foie gras in quality. Duck and turkey also are eaten, especially for special holiday dinners. Hunting is a common pastime, and rabbit, venison, and assorted small game frequently appear on the menu.

Lake Balaton, the largest warm-water lake in Central Europe, lies in Transdanubia. It provides over 50 species of freshwater fish, eaten by the people of the area. "Fogas," a species of pike perch, is unique to the lake. Carp and sturgeon also are eaten. Trout, caught in the numerous rivers, are prepared in several delicious ways.

Vegetables are popular in Hungary. Spring, summer, and autumn provide a bounty of fresh vegetables of many varieties. The thrifty Hungarian housewife preserves many vegetables for winter consumption. Sauerkraut is homemade in large quantities, and whole heads of cabbage are also pickled and used for stuffed cabbage. Lecsó is prepared and canned for winter use with meats. Herbs are dried, and onions and garlic are hung for winter use. Among the vegetables preferred by Hungarian cooks are red cabbage, cauliflower, beans, cabbage, mushrooms, peppers, and zucchini. Vegetables are frequently stuffed, and many are prepared in rich sauces. Salads are popular in summer and are generally served as a side dish with the main meal.

Many fruits are grown. Apricots, cherries, plums, apples, and grapes are served fresh, preserved, or prepared in fine pastries. Wheat is the most popular grain, and the rolling plains of Hungary supply the grain not only for herself but for much of Central Europe. Corn and rye also are used. Home-baked bread is the rule rather than the exception. Noodles, dumplings, and pancakes, both sweet and savory, are staples of the Hungarian diet. Delicious tortes and strudels are made with high-quality Hungarian flour especially suited for baking, owing to its high gluten content.

Within Hungarian cuisine today there remain two different and distinct cooking styles. The cooking of the upper classes and the court cuisine mimics the cooking of France, Austria, and Germany in many of its dishes. The second cooking style is that of the Hungarian peasant which is by far the more innovative of the two styles.

Technique is the hallmark of fine Hungarian cooking. Several basic techniques occur again and again in a variety of dishes, giving them that character that we define as Hungarian. Lard is used in preference to any other fat. It is rendered when the pigs are slaughtered and used throughout the year. Goose fat is also rendered and used interchangeably with lard. Onion is fried in the lard until golden to impart color and aroma to many dishes. The pan is then removed from the heat, and paprika is added. Paprika is high in sugar content and will scorch if cooked over high heat. Most Hungarian stews and some soups begin with this technique. Dishes are thickened at the end of cooking. Flour and sour cream are mixed together and added just before serving. A roux is often made with lard and flour and then lightly browned. This is often added to soups.

The soups and stews so important to Hungarian cooking can be traced back to the Magyar heritage. Hungarian cooking has raised these dishes to a very high level of sophistication. Four basic categories are often used and have the following familiar characteristics: *Gulyas* refers to a soup always containing paprika. It may also contain vegetables. *Porkölt* is a meat dish in which the meat is cooked in very little liquid. Beef, pork, or lamb is generally used. This dish begins with the classic onion cooked in lard with paprika added. The dish may also contain peppers. It is the dish closest to what we call goulash. *Paprikas* is generally made with chicken or veal. It always contains paprika and is thickened with sour cream and flour. *Tokany* is a ragout or stew in which the meat is cooked in very little liquid and vegetables are added. It is generally seasoned with marjoram. Within each category there are numerous variations, dependent solely upon the cook.

Paprika is the single most important spice in the Hungarian kitchen. Interestingly enough, it was not used in Hungary until the sixteenth century. The pepper is a form of capsicum, the same botanical genus as potatoes and tomatoes. There is a great deal of controversy as to how paprika was brought to Hungary. The two most probable explanations are: paprika was brought by the Turks from the Middle East or the peppers were brought by Columbus from the New World and were introduced into Hungary from the European courts.

Several hundred varieties of peppers are now grown. The seeds and veins are removed from the dried peppers, and the peppers are then ground to a fine powder. There are six standardized strengths of paprika, ranging from the sweet ''Noble Rose'' paprika to a hot paprika much like cayenne. The most readily available, authentic Hungarian paprika is the ''Noble Rose'' which is the one used in this book. It would appear that paprika was indeed a beneficial discovery for the Hungarian population, since it has been found to be a rich source of vitamins A and C, adding both spice and nutrition to the peasant diet. Few other spices are used in Hungarian cooking; however, caraway, dill, thyme, marjoram, and black pepper are occasionally used.

Meals are an important family gathering time in Hungary. Breakfast is eaten early and generally consists of sliced sausages or meats, cheese, and bread and perhaps fruit brandy in the dead of winter. The noon meal is the main meal of the day. A thick, hearty soup generally begins the meal, frequently containing noodles or dumplings. Appetizers are not commonly eaten in Hungary, but many of the dishes served as main courses or accompaniments are easily adapted for a delicious hors d'oeuvre. The main course follows the soup, accompanied by fresh bread and salad or vegetables in season. Dessert is often noodles or dumplings either sweet or savory in nature. Sweet cakes and pastries are generally reserved for special occasions. Coffee and pastries are served in the late afternoon in the cities. Supper is light and generally served late.

Hungarian cooking offers a wide variety of dishes that are both highly creative and inexpensive to prepare. The recipes offer a great deal of adaptability, suitable for many different meals. Try some of the following recipes as an introduction to some of the delicious dishes that Hungarian cuisine has to offer, and I am sure you will enjoy them!

soups and appetizers

bean soup

1 cup dried white beans
1 ham hock or ham bone
8 cups water
1 bay leaf
1 carrot, diced
2 stalks celery, sliced
1 clove garlic, mashed

1 tablespoon lard
1 medium onion, peeled, chopped
1 tablespoon flour
1½ teaspoons sweet paprika
½ pound smoked sausage
   (Debrecziner or Kielbasi are good
   choices)

Wash beans; pick over, removing foreign matter. Place in small bowl. Cover with water; soak overnight.

Following day place beans, remaining water, and ham bone in Dutch oven. Add 8 cups water and bay leaf. Bring to boil; cover. Reduce heat to low; cook, stirring occasionally, 2½ to 3 hours or until beans are tender. Remove ham hock. Take meat from bone; dice. Return meat to soup. Add carrot, celery, and garlic; cook 30 minutes.

Meanwhile melt lard in small heavy skillet. Add onion; cook until transparent. Add flour; reduce heat to very low. Cook, stirring, until flour is lightly and evenly browned. Remove from heat; stir in paprika. Ladle 1 cup soup into roux; mix well. Add mixture to soup; mix thoroughly. Add sausage; cook, stirring occasionally, until soup thickens. Taste; adjust seasonings if necessary. Pinched noodles (*csipetke*) can be added to this soup if desired.

Garnish soup with spoonful sour cream. Serve with crusty bread and chopped onions. Makes 6 servings.

caraway soup

garlic croutons
3 slices firm white bread (rye or black bread can be substituted)
3 tablespoons bacon fat or butter
1 clove garlic, peeled

Trim crusts from bread; cut into ½-inch cubes.

Melt butter in small frying pan. Add garlic; sauté until lightly browned. Remove; discard. Add bread cubes; cook, stirring, until golden. Drain on absorbent paper. Set aside; keep warm.

soup
4 tablespoons lard or bacon fat
1 tablespoon caraway seeds
4 tablespoons flour
1½ teaspoons salt
⅛ teaspoon pepper
6 cups water
1 egg, well-beaten

Melt lard in large saucepan. Add caraway seeds and flour; cook, stirring constantly, over low heat until lightly browned. Remove from heat. Add salt, pepper, and water; stir until well-blended. Return to heat; cook, stirring, until thickened.

Add ½ cup soup to egg; beat well. Add to pot; cook, stirring, 4 minutes.

Serve soup in individual bowls; garnish with croutons. Makes 4 servings.

chicken and vegetable soup with pinched noodles

2 tablespoons butter or margarine
2 carrots, peeled, sliced
2 stalks celery, sliced
½ cup chopped green pepper
1 small onion, peeled, chopped
4 cups chicken broth or stock (preferably homemade; see Index)
1½ cups chopped cooked chicken or turkey
1 large tomato, peeled, chopped
Salt and pepper
½ cup frozen peas
½ recipe Pinched Noodles (see Index)

Heat butter in large saucepan. Add carrots, celery, green pepper, and onion; sauté 6 minutes, stirring occasionally. Add chicken broth, chicken, tomato, salt, and pepper; cook 20 minutes. Add peas; stir well. Cook 5 minutes. Add small pieces of noodles; cook 5 minutes, stirring occasionally. Makes 4 servings.

variation
Omit pinched noodles; add ¼ cup raw long-grain rice to soup when chicken broth is added.

Note: Save carcass from roast chicken; use to make stock for above soup. Add leftover meat to broth.

cold cherry soup

1 pound fresh sour cherries
¾ cup sugar
4 cups water
1 cinnamon stick (3 inches long)
2 strips lemon rind
¼ teaspoon salt
½ cup cold water
2 tablespoons cornstarch
½ cup dry red wine
¾ cup sour cream

Wash cherries well. Remove the stems; pit cherries. Place in large saucepan with sugar, 4 cups water, cinnamon, lemon rind, and salt. Bring to boil over moderate heat; cover. Reduce heat to low; cook 10 minutes. Remove cinnamon stick and lemon rind.

Combine cold water and cornstarch; mix well. Add slowly to soup; mix well. Cook, stirring, until slightly thickened. Remove from heat; stir in wine.

Place sour cream in small bowl. Add 1 cup hot soup; mix well. Pour mixture into saucepan; mix thoroughly. Place in covered container; chill well.

Serve soup in chilled bowls. Garnish with sour cream; and sprinkle lightly with cinnamon. Makes 6 servings.

sauerkraut soup

This dish is traditionally considered a hangover cure and is served at the end of a New Year's Eve party.

2 tablespoons lard
½ pound lean boneless pork
1 medium onion, chopped
2 teaspoons Hungarian sweet paprika
4 cups water
Salt and pepper
1 16-ounce can sauerkraut
½ pound Polish sausage, sliced
2 tablespoons flour
2 tablespoons water
Sour cream

Heat lard in large saucepan. Add pork; cook over moderate heat until well-browned. Remove with slotted spoon; reserve. Add onion; cook until transparent. Remove from heat; add paprika, stirring well. Add water, salt, pepper, and reserved pork. Cover; bring to boil over moderate heat. Reduce heat to low; cook 1½ hours or until meat is tender. Add sauerkraut and sausage; cook 20 minutes. (Rinse sauerkraut if less-tart soup is desired.)

Combine flour and water; mix well. Add to soup; cook, stirring, until slightly thickened.

Serve soup in individual bowls; top with dollop of sour cream. Makes 4 to 5 servings.

giblet soup

½ cup flour
2½ teaspoons salt
¼ teaspoon pepper
½ teaspoon paprika
½ teaspoon poultry seasoning
1 teaspoon parsley flakes
½ pound chicken gizzards
¼ pound chicken livers
1 pound chicken necks
4 tablespoons bacon drippings
10 cups water
1 small onion, studded with 2 cloves
2 celery stalks with leaves, chopped
2 tablespoons butter or margarine
½ cup chopped onion
2 carrots, peeled, diced
2 stalks celery, chopped
1 cup chopped tomatoes
Salt and pepper

Combine flour, ½ teaspoon salt, pepper, paprika, poultry seasoning, and parsley flakes.

Wash chicken gizzards, livers, and necks. Dredge chicken parts well in flour mixture.

Heat bacon fat in Dutch oven. Fry chicken in fat until well-browned. Remove livers; reserve. Add water, onion, 2 stalks celery, and 2 teaspoons salt to pan; bring to boil. Cover; reduce heat to low; cook 1 hour. Add livers; cook 30 minutes. Strain broth. Cool gizzards, livers, and necks.

Wash Dutch oven. Return to heat; melt butter. Add onion, carrots, and 2 stalks celery; cook until tender. Add broth, tomatoes, salt, and pepper; bring to boil. Cover; reduce heat to low; cook 30 minutes.

Meanwhile, finely mince gizzards and livers. Pick neck bones; chop meat. Add chopped chicken and giblets to soup; heat through. Makes 6 servings.

potato soup

3 tablespoons bacon fat or lard
1 medium onion, chopped fine
1½ tablespoons flour
1 stalk celery, chopped
1 carrot, peeled, chopped
½ cup minced green pepper
1 pound potatoes, peeled, diced
6 cups water or vegetable stock
1 teaspoon Hungarian paprika
1½ teaspoons salt
Pepper

Heat fat in large saucepan or Dutch oven. Add onion; cook until transparent. Add flour; cook, stirring, until lightly browned. Add remaining ingredients; stir well. Bring to boil; cover. Reduce heat to low; cook 40 minutes or until vegetables are tender. Pinched Noodles (see Index) or Dumplings (see Index) can be added to soup if desired, or several cut-up frankfurters can be added. Makes 4 servings.

gulyas soup

1 pound lean boneless stewing beef
2 tablespoons lard
2 medium onions, peeled, chopped
1 clove garlic, peeled, chopped
2 teaspoons Hungarian sweet paprika
Dash of cayenne pepper
3 cups beef stock or broth
2 cups water
½ teaspoon caraway seeds
½ teaspoon crumbled dried marjoram
Salt and pepper
1 16-ounce can tomatoes, broken up
2 medium potatoes, peeled, diced
2 medium carrots, peeled, sliced
2 red sweet peppers, cleaned, cut into chunks (green peppers may
   be substituted all or in part)
2 tablespoons flour
2 tablespoons water
Sour cream

Wipe beef with damp cloth; cut into 1-inch cubes.

Melt lard in Dutch oven. Add beef; brown well on all sides. Remove from pan with slotted spoon; reserve.

Add onions and garlic to pan; cook 4 minutes, stirring occasionally. Add paprika, cayenne, stock, 2 cups water, caraway, marjoram, salt, pepper and reserved meat. Stir well. Bring to boil over moderate heat. Reduce heat to low and cook, covered, 45 minutes. Add tomatoes, potatoes, carrots, and red peppers. Stir well; return to boil. Cover; cook 30 minutes.

Combine flour and 2 tablespoons water; stir to form smooth paste. Add slowly to soup, stirring well. Cook over low heat, stirring until thickened.

Serve soup in individual bowls; top with sour cream. Makes 4 to 5 servings.

Picture on opposite page: gulyas soup

broth with liver dumplings

4 chicken livers
½ small onion
1 tablespoon chicken fat or soft butter
1 egg, beaten
½ teaspoon crumbled dried marjoram
1 tablespoon chopped parsley
Salt and pepper
1 tablespoon flour
Approximately 3 tablespoons dry bread crumbs
5 cups beef or chicken broth

Put livers and onion through food grinder, or chop in food processor. Add fat, egg, and seasonings; mix well. Add flour and bread crumbs; mix. Add enough bread crumbs to form stiff mixture. Refrigerate 1 hour.

Heat broth to boiling in medium saucepan.

Form liver mixture into walnut-size dumplings. Drop into boiling soup; do not crowd. Cook 10 minutes or until dumplings float. Remove with slotted spoon; place in warm soup tureen. Continue until all dumplings are cooked. Strain broth over dumplings.

Serve soup garnished with chopped parsley. Makes 4 servings.

broth with liver dumplings

mushroom turnovers

1 cup butter
1 8-ounce package cream cheese
2 cups flour

½ teaspoon salt
1 egg, well-beaten

mushroom filling
2 tablespoons butter or margarine
½ cup sliced green onions
½ pound mushrooms, cleaned, chopped
½ teaspoon salt

⅛ teaspoon pepper
1 teaspoon lemon juice
1 teaspoon flour
½ cup sour cream

Allow butter and cream cheese to stand at room temperature 1 hour to soften.

Place butter and cream cheese in mixing bowl; beat until light. Add flour and salt; mix well. Form into ball. Cover; chill overnight.

Prepare Mushroom Filling. Melt butter in heavy skillet. Add onions and mushrooms; cook until mushrooms are lightly browned and liquid has evaporated. Add salt, pepper, and lemon juice; stir well. Stir in flour and sour cream; cook over very low heat until thickened. Allow to cool before rolling dough.

Remove dough from refrigerator few minutes before rolling. Divide into 3 parts. Roll 1 part at a time on lightly floured board to ⅛ inch thick. Cut into 2½ inch rounds. Place 1 teaspoon filling in center of each round. Moisten edges with water. Fold in half; crimp edges. Reroll trimmings. Place on ungreased baking sheet; brush with beaten egg. Bake in preheated 350°F oven 25 to 30 minutes. Makes 5 to 6 dozen appetizers.

deviled eggs

6 hard-cooked eggs
2 tablespoons mayonnaise
3 tablespoons tomato catsup
½ teaspoon dry mustard
½ teaspoon lemon juice

Few drops of Tabasco
¼ teaspoon salt
White pepper
Paprika
Finely chopped green onion

Peel eggs; cut in half lengthwise. Place yolks in small bowl. Add remaining ingredients, except paprika and onion; mix well. Spoon mixture into egg whites, or use decorating tube and pipe egg-yolk mixture into whites. Sprinkle with paprika and onion. Refrigerate until serving time. Makes 4 servings as an appetizer.

deviled eggs with bacon

Omit catsup; add 3 tablespoons sour cream and 2 slices crisp bacon, crumbled. Proceed as in above recipe.

caraway biscuits with ham filling

1 10-ounce package pie-crust mix
½ cup shredded Swiss cheese
4 tablespoons cold water (approximately)
1 egg, well-beaten
1 tablespoon caraway seeds

ham filling
1¼ cups ground or finely minced cooked ham
¼ cup mayonnaise
¼ cup finely minced celery
1½ teaspoons freeze-dried chives
½ teaspoon prepared mustard

Combine pie-crust mix and Swiss cheese in mixing bowl; mix well. Sprinkle cold water over mix; stir with fork until mixture is just dampened. Form into ball. If mixture will not hold together, add small amount cold water. Divide dough into 2 parts; roll 1 part at a time on pastry cloth or lightly floured surface to ¼ inch thick. Cut into 1½-inch rounds (approximately 40). Place on ungreased cookie sheets. Brush half of rounds with egg; sprinkle lightly with caraway seeds. Bake in preheated 375°F oven 10 to 12 minutes or until lightly browned. Place on rack to cool.

Combine all filling ingredients; mix well. Place heaping teaspoons of mixture on plain pie-crust rounds; top each with caraway-seed-topped round.

Arrange biscuits on platter; garnish with parsley and cherry tomatoes. Makes approximately 20 appetizers.

Note: Pie-crust rounds can be made in advance and stored in airtight container until ready for use.

deviled eggs

13

appetizer strudel

appetizer strudel

3 tablespoons bacon fat or lard
3 cups shredded cabbage
1 small onion, grated
1½ teaspoons caraway seeds
Salt and pepper

3 sheets phyllo or strudel leaves
   (available in delicatessens)
3 tablespoons melted butter
1 tablespoon fine dry bread crumbs
1 egg yolk, well-beaten

Melt fat in large heavy skillet. Add cabbage and onion; cook, stirring, until limp. Add caraway seeds and salt and pepper to taste. Set aside.

Set out large clean linen towel. Remove strudel leaves from package; immediately cover with very lightly dampened towel and plastic wrap to prevent drying. Place 1 strudel leaf on towel, long side toward you. (Strudel leaves are usually rectangular in shape.) Brush with melted butter; sprinkle with ½ tablespoon bread crumbs. Top with second strudel leaf. Brush with butter; sprinkle with crumbs. Top with third strudel leaf; brush with butter. Arrange cabbage filling on dough in 3-inch-wide band, 1 inch from edge of dough, leaving 1½ inches free on both ends. Roll up like jelly roll, using towel to support dough. Carefully transfer to lightly greased baking sheet. Turn ends under to seal. Cut several slits in top of dough. Brush with beaten egg. Bake in preheated 375°F oven 25 minutes or until golden. Carefully remove from cookie sheet; cut into 6 pieces. Makes 6 servings.

variations

Can also be filled with mushrooms and sour cream or any leftover minced meat preparation, such as chicken paprikas. Take care not to use too much gravy.

14

fish dishes

pan-fried
fish fillets

1 pound frozen firm whitefish fillets (such as flounder. haddock, or sole)
2 eggs
2 tablespoons milk
¾ cup fine dry bread crumbs
½ teaspoon Hungarian sweet paprika
1 teaspoon dried parsley flakes
Salt and pepper
4 tablespoons butter or margarine
2 tablespoons lemon juice
1 tablespoon chopped parsley

Defrost fish. Drain well; pat dry.

Beat eggs and milk together in shallow bowl; set aside.

Combine bread crumbs and seasonings on waxed paper; mix well.

Heat 2 tablespoons butter in heavy skillet.

Dip fish in egg mixture, then in crumbs, coating well; shake off excess. Fry in hot butter over moderate heat until golden; turn once. Drain on absorbent paper. Add more butter as needed; continue until all fillets are cooked. Keep warm. Add lemon juice and parsley to skillet; stir well. Pour over fish. Makes 4 servings.

fish fillets with walnut sauce

3½ cups water
½ cup dry white wine
¼ cup coarsely chopped celery
2 sprigs parsley
2 cloves
1 bay leaf
1 slice lemon
¾ teaspoon salt
1 pound whitefish fillets, defrosted if frozen

walnut sauce
1½ tablespoons butter or margarine
1½ tablespoons flour
Salt and pepper
¾ cup reserved fish stock
¼ cup sour cream

¼ cup toasted walnuts
Chopped parsley

Combine water, wine, vegetables, and seasonings in large saucepan; bring to boil. Reduce heat to low; cook 25 minutes. Strain liquid into large shallow skillet; bring to boil. Add fish pieces; cover. Simmer 5 to 6 minutes or until fish flakes easily. Carefully transfer to platter; keep warm while making sauce.

Melt butter in small saucepan. Add flour, salt, and pepper; cook over low heat until bubbly. Add reserved fish stock slowly, stirring constantly; cook over low heat until thickened. Remove from heat; add sour cream, stirring well.

Pour sauce over fish; sprinkle with toasted walnuts and a little chopped parsley. Serve with steamed potatoes or rice. Makes 4 servings.

sautéed brook trout

4 whole trout, cleaned (5 to 7 ounces each)
¼ cup flour
Salt and pepper
6 tablespoons butter
3 tablespoons cooking oil
¼ cup coarsely chopped walnuts
Juice of ½ lemon
2 tablespoons finely chopped parsley

Wash trout well; pat dry.

Combine flour, salt, and pepper; dredge fish in mixture.

Heat 3 tablespoons butter and oil in large heavy skillet until foam subsides. Add trout; cook 4 minutes over medium-high heat. Fish should be well-browned. Turn; cook until fish flakes easily. Carefully transfer to warm platter.

Pour off any fat remaining in pan; wipe out pan with paper towel. Add remaining butter; cook over low heat until melted. Add walnuts; sauté 3 minutes. Add lemon juice and parsley; pour over fish.

Serve trout with boiled or steamed potatoes. Makes 4 servings.

fish fillets baked with sour cream

1 pound firm whitefish fillets
Salt and pepper
½ cup sour cream
1½ tablespoons Parmesan cheese
¾ teaspoon Hungarian sweet paprika
¼ teaspoon crumbled tarragon
2 tablespoons seasoned bread crumbs
2 tablespoons butter or margarine
Finely chopped parsley
Lemon wedges

Arrange fish in single layer in lightly greased shallow baking dish. Season with salt and pepper.

Combine sour cream, cheese, paprika, and tarragon; mix well. Spread evenly over fillets. Sprinkle with bread crumbs; dot with butter. Bake in preheated 350°F oven 20 to 25 minutes or until fish flakes easily.

Sprinkle fish with parsley; serve with lemon wedges. Makes 4 servings.

fishermen's soup

2 tablespoons lard
2 medium onions, peeled, chopped
2½ to 3 pounds freshwater fish (trout, pike, and bass); use one or more kind of fish, as desired
1 quart water
1 teaspoon salt
1 tablespoon Hungarian sweet paprika

Melt lard in Dutch oven. Add onions; cook until tender and lightly browned.

Clean and bone fish, reserving heads and bones. Cut fish into 2-inch pieces. Add fish trimmings, water, and salt to Dutch oven. Stir well; bring to boil. Reduce heat to low; cover pan. Simmer 20 minutes.

Strain broth; return to Dutch oven. Add paprika; stir well. Add fish. Simmer, uncovered, 20 minutes, shaking pan occasionally. Do not stir; fish pieces will break.

Serve soup hot in individual bowls with crusty bread. Makes 4 servings.

hungarian-style fish fillet

1 pound firm whitefish fillets, defrosted if frozen
Juice of 1 lemon
3 slices bacon, diced
2 tablespoons lard
2 tablespoons flour
Salt and pepper
2 small peppers (1 green and 1 red), cleaned, cut into ½-inch strips
1 large onion, peeled, sliced
1 medium cucumber (unpeeled), thinly sliced
White pepper
½ teaspoon Hungarian sweet paprika
¼ cup finely chopped parsley
4 lemon wedges

Rinse fish; pat dry. Place in shallow bowl; sprinkle with lemon juice. Let stand 10 minutes.

Place bacon in large heavy skillet; cook over moderate heat until crisp. Remove bacon with slotted spoon.

Add lard to skillet; melt.

Combine flour and salt and pepper to taste.

Drain fish; dredge in flour mixture. Brown fish in hot fat, turning once. Remove to hot platter.

Add peppers, onion, and cucumber to skillet; sauté until tender, stirring frequently. Add salt, white pepper, and paprika; stir well. Spoon over fish.

Sprinkle fish with reserved bacon and parsley; garnish with lemon wedges. Makes 4 servings.

halibut with tomato sauce

2 tablespoons lard
1 cup chopped onion
1 clove garlic, peeled, minced
Salt and white pepper
1 16-ounce can tomatoes, drained, chopped
Dash of Tabasco
2 tablespoons dry sherry
2 tablespoons finely chopped parsley
4 halibut steaks, approximately 6 ounces each
4 tablespoons lemon juice
2 tablespoons butter or margarine

First make sauce. Melt lard in small skillet over moderate heat. Add onion; cook 3 minutes. Add garlic; cook until onion is lightly browned. Add salt, pepper, tomatoes, and Tabasco. Cover; simmer 15 minutes. Keep warm while cooking fish. Stir in sherry and parsley just before pouring over fish.

Rub fish steaks with 2 tablespoons lemon juice; let stand 10 minutes. Place on preheated, lightly greased broiler pan; brush with remaining lemon juice and butter. Broil 6 inches from heat source 5 to 6 minutes per side; baste once. Turn; cook 5 minutes. Transfer fish to warm platter.

Pour sauce over fish. Serve with boiled potatoes. Makes 4 servings.

hungarian-style fish fillet

halibut with tomato sauce

fish goulash esterhazy

1 pound firm whitefish fillets (pike,
   perch, or carp, if available, are good)
Juice of 1 lemon

broth
2 tablespoons lard
1 medium onion, peeled, sliced
2 carrots, peeled, sliced
2 tablespoons chopped parsley
1 bay leaf
$1/8$ teaspoon crumbled dried marjoram
3 slices lemon
Salt and pepper
4 cups water

vegetables
1 cup chicken broth
3 medium carrots, peeled, cut into
   matchstick strips
1 stalk celery, cut into matchstick strips

sauce
2 tablespoons lard
2 tablespoons flour
2 teaspoons Hungarian sweet paprika
Salt and white pepper
$1\frac{1}{2}$ cups reserved fish broth
$1/2$ cup sour cream
1 tablespoon chopped capers

fish goulash esterházy

Wash fish; pat dry. Cut into serving-size pieces; place in shallow
bowl. Sprinkle with lemon juice; refrigerate until needed.

Heat 2 tablespoons lard in large shallow skillet. Add onion and
sliced carrots; cook until limp. Add remaining broth ingredients;
bring to boil. Reduce heat to low; cook 20 minutes. Strain broth;
return to skillet. Bring to boil.

Drain fish; add to skillet. Cover; reduce heat to low; cook 20 minutes or until fish flakes easily. Reserve broth; strain.

Place broth in small saucepan; bring to boil. Add matchstick vegetables. Reduce heat to low; cook 10 minutes. Drain; keep warm.

Make sauce. Melt lard in medium saucepan. Add flour; cook until
bubbly. Remove from heat; stir in paprika, salt, and pepper. Add
fish broth. Return to heat; cook, stirring constantly, until thickened. Stir in sour cream and capers; cook over very low heat until
heated through.

Arrange fish in serving dish. Pour sauce over fish; garnish with
matchstick vegetables. Serve immediately with crusty bread. Makes
4 servings.

20

meat dishes

stuffed cabbage rolls

1 pound lean ground beef
1 medium onion, chopped
½ cup raw long-grain rice
½ cup sour cream
½ teaspoon garlic powder
Salt and pepper
1 large head cabbage
1 1-pound can sauerkraut (do not drain)
1 16-ounce can tomatoes, pureed or sieved
1 bay leaf
Sour cream

Combine beef, onion, rice, ½ cup sour cream, garlic powder, salt, and pepper in mixing bowl; mix well. Set aside.

Core cabbage; under running water, remove 12 to 15 leaves (depending on size of leaves). Discard limp or damaged leaves.

Bring 2 inches of water to boil in Dutch oven. Add cabbage leaves; steam until limp (about 10 minutes); drain well. Place 2 to 3 tablespoons filling on each cabbage leaf. Fold sides of cabbage leaf to center; roll. Secure with wooden picks.

Shred any cabbage remaining from cabbage head.

Place sauerkraut in bottom of Dutch oven. Add shredded cabbage; top with cabbage rolls.

Combine tomatoes, salt, and pepper; pour over cabbage rolls. Add bay leaf. Place heavy plate on cabbage rolls. (This weights down cabbage rolls so they stay under liquid as they cook.) Cover; bring to boil. Reduce heat to low; cook 1 hour.

Top rolls with sour cream; serve with sauerkraut and cabbage. Makes 4 servings.

pork chops with ham and capers

pork chops with ham and capers

4 loin pork chops, 1 inch thick
2 tablespoons lemon juice
Salt and pepper
2 tablespoons lard
½ cup chicken broth
¼ cup white wine
2 ounces boiled ham, cut into julienne strips
2 tablespoons finely chopped sweet pickle
1 tablespoon coarsely chopped capers
½ cup sour cream
1 tablespoon flour

Wipe pork with damp cloth. Rub with lemon juice, salt, and pepper; let stand 10 minutes.

Heat lard in heavy skillet. Add chops; brown well on both sides over moderate heat. Add broth and wine; cook, covered, over low heat 30 to 35 minutes or until done through. Remove to platter; keep warm.

Add ham, pickle, and capers to liquid in skillet; cook 3 minutes.

Combine sour cream and flour; stir well. Add to sauce, stirring constantly. Cook over very low heat until thickened.

Pour sauce over the chops. Makes 4 servings.

veal fricassee

1½ pounds cubed veal shoulder or leg
4 tablespoons butter
½ cup chopped onion
Salt and pepper
2 cups water
2 teaspoons instant chicken-broth granules
2 carrots, peeled, sliced
2 stalks celery, sliced
¾ cup sliced fresh mushrooms
1 tablespoon chopped parsley
2 tablespoons flour
1 tablespoon lemon juice

Wipe veal with damp cloth.

Melt 2 tablespoons butter in heavy saucepan. Add veal; brown lightly on all sides. Push meat to side of pan. Add onion; cook until lightly browned. Add salt, pepper, water, and chicken-broth granules; bring to boil. Cover; cook over low heat 1 hour. Add carrots and celery; cook 15 minutes. Add mushrooms and parsley; cook 10 minutes.

Meanwhile melt 2 tablespoons butter in small saucepan. Add flour; cook over low heat, stirring to form lightly browned roux.

Remove meat and vegetables from heat. Drain liquid from stew; add enough hot water (if necessary) to make 1½ cups. Add broth slowly to roux, stirring well; cook over low heat until thickened. Stir sauce and lemon juice into meat and vegetables.

Serve veal with rice or boiled potatoes. Makes 4 servings.

Note: Any combination of vegetables can be substituted for carrots and celery in this recipe. Cauliflower or peas are often used.

beef steak esterházy

1½ pounds beef round steak, cut into 4 pieces
2 tablespoons lard
1 medium onion, peeled, chopped
1 carrot, peeled, chopped
1 stalk celery, chopped
1 parsnip, peeled, chopped
1½ cups beef broth or stock
½ teaspoon grated lemon rind
1 bay leaf
Salt and pepper

2 tablespoons butter or margarine
1 carrot, peeled, cut into matchstick strips
1 stalk celery, cut into matchstick strips
1 parsnip, peeled, cut into matchstick strips
2 tablespoons boiling water
1 teaspoon sharp prepared mustard
2 tablespoons flour
½ cup heavy cream

Wipe steaks with damp cloth.

Heat lard in large heavy skillet. Brown beef well on both sides. Remove from pan.

Add chopped vegetables to pan; sauté until tender. Add broth, lemon rind, bay leaf, salt, and pepper; mix well. Add steaks. Bring to boil; cover. Reduce heat to low; cook 1¼ to 1½ hours or until the steak is tender.

Meanwhile melt butter in medium saucepan. Add vegetable strips and 2 tablespoons boiling water; cover. Cook over low heat until tender, adding more water if needed; reserve.

Transfer steak to platter; keep warm. Remove bay leaf from pan; discard. Puree broth and chopped vegetables in electric blender, or force through sieve; return to pan. Stir in mustard; cook over moderate heat until bubbly.

Mix flour with 2 tablespoons water to form smooth paste. Stir into gravy; cook, stirring constantly, until thickened. Remove from heat; stir in cream. Cook over very low heat 3 to 4 minutes.

Pour sauce over steaks; garnish with matchstick vegetables. Makes 4 servings.

pork and sauerkraut goulash

1¼ pounds lean pork, cut into 1½-inch cubes
¼ cup flour
¾ teaspoon salt
¼ teaspoon pepper
¼ cup lard or bacon drippings
1 medium onion, peeled, chopped

1 green pepper, cut into strips
1½ teaspoons Hungarian sweet paprika
1 cup beef broth
1 16-ounce can sauerkraut, drained
Sour cream for garnish

Trim pork of excess fat; wipe with damp cloth.

Combine flour, salt, and pepper. Dredge meat in mixture.

Heat lard in large heavy saucepan or Dutch oven. Brown meat well on all sides. Remove with slotted spoon; reserve.

Add onion and green pepper to fat; cook until onion is tender. Drain off remaining fat. Add paprika, broth, and browned pork; bring to boil. Reduce heat to low; cook, covered, 50 minutes. Add sauerkraut; cook 45 minutes.

Garnish with sour cream; serve with Noodles (see Index). Makes 4 servings.

stuffed peppers

4 large green peppers
Boiling salted water
1 pound ground pork
1 medium onion, peeled, chopped
1 clove garlic, minced
1 teaspoon Hungarian
   sweet paprika

Salt and pepper
1 16-ounce can stewed tomatoes
1 8-ounce can tomato sauce
¼ cup water
1 cup instant rice (quick-cooking)

Cut tops from peppers; remove seeds and veins. Leave peppers whole. Place peppers in 1 inch boiling salted water; steam, covered, 5 minutes over low heat. Drain well.

Meanwhile brown pork over moderate heat in heavy skillet. Add fat only if meat is very lean. Add onion and garlic when meat is half-cooked. Stir occasionally to ensure even browning. Drain off fat; remove from heat. Add paprika, salt, pepper, stewed tomatoes, half of tomato sauce, and water; mix well. Stir in rice; bring to boil over moderate heat. Reduce heat to low; cook 15 minutes.

Place peppers upright in 1½-quart casserole. Fill with meat and rice mixture; spoon any remaining meat and rice around peppers. Spoon remaining tomato sauce over peppers; cover. Bake at 350°F 30 minutes. Uncover; cook 10 minutes.

Top with grated cheese if desired. Serve with bread or rolls. Makes 4 servings.

robber's meat

This dish is traditionally cooked over a charcoal fire and is still available in many country csardas today.

2 pounds lean lamb, cut into 1½-inch cubes

marinade

¼ cup chopped onion
1 clove garlic, crushed
3 tablespoons cooking oil
1½ tablespoons red wine vinegar

½ teaspoon crumbled dried
   marjoram
Salt and pepper

2 green peppers, cleaned, cut into chunks
2 onions, peeled, cut into chunks
½ pound fresh mushrooms, cleaned, stems removed

Wipe meat with damp cloth; place in glass bowl or casserole.

Combine all marinade ingredients; pour over meat. Mix well; cover. Refrigerate overnight.

Lightly oil 4 long skewers.

Drain meat; reserve marinade.

Thread meat and vegetables alternately on skewers. Brush with marinade.

Build standard charcoal fire in outdoor barbecue. When coals are white-hot, grill meat 4 inches from coals; allow approximately 10 minutes per side. Brush occasionally with marinade. Slide off skewers.

Serve meat with crisp cabbage salad and fried potatoes. Makes 4 servings.

Note: Beef or pork or any combination of these meats can be used for Robber's Meat.

beef gulyas

3 slices bacon, diced
½ cup chopped onion
1½ pounds stew beef, cut into 1½-inch cubes
2 to 3 teaspoons Hungarian sweet paprika
½ teaspoon crushed caraway seeds
Salt and pepper
2 cups beef broth
2 cups frozen small pearl onions
1½ tablespoons flour
1½ tablespoons water

Cook bacon in large heavy skillet until crisp. Remove with slotted spoon; reserve.

Add onion to skillet; cook until tender. Reserve.

Add beef to skillet; brown well on all sides. Remove from heat. Add paprika, caraway seeds, salt, and pepper; stir well. Add reserved onion and broth. Return to heat. Cover; bring to boil over moderate heat. Reduce heat to low; cook 1½ hours. Add pearl onions and bacon; cook 45 minutes to 1 hour or until tender.

Combine flour and water; stir to form smooth paste. Slowly stir into stew; cook, stirring constantly, until thickened.

Garnish gulyas with sour cream or sautéed green peppers; accompany with buttered noodles. Makes 4 servings.

stuffed kohlrabi

8 medium kohlrabi
2 tablespoons butter or margarine
½ cup chopped onion
½ pound ground veal
½ pound ground pork
1 egg, well-beaten

2 tablespoons bread crumbs
1 tablespoon chopped parsley
½ teaspoon crumbled dried marjoram
Salt and white pepper
2 cups hot chicken broth

sauce

3 tablespoons butter
3 tablespoons flour
Salt and white pepper

¼ cup heavy cream
2 tablespoons chopped fresh parsley

Wash kohlrabi. Cut off leaves and stems; reserve. Peel root. Cut ½-inch slice (reserve slices); scoop out pulp, leaving ¼-inch shell. Chop pulp. Select tender leaves; shred. Place leaves and pulp in Dutch oven.

Melt butter in small saucepan. Add onion; sauté until tender.

Combine veal, pork, egg, bread crumbs, parsley, and seasonings in mixing bowl. Add onion; mix well. Pack mixture into kohlrabi shells, mounding slightly. Top with slice removed in first step. Place in Dutch oven. Pour broth over kohlrabi; bring to boil. Cover; reduce heat to low. Simmer 30 to 40 minutes or until shells can be pierced with fork. Transfer kohlrabi to baking dish. Strain broth; reserve. Place cooked kohlrabi leaves around stuffed kohlrabi; keep warm.

Prepare sauce. Melt butter in medium saucepan. Add flour, salt, and pepper; cook, stirring, until bubbly. Add 1½ cups reserved broth; cook over low heat until thickened. Remove from heat; stir in cream. Pour over kohlrabi; sprinkle with parsley. Broil in oven until sauce is lightly browned. Serve immediately. Makes 4 servings.

braised steak tapé

1¼ pounds sliced round steak
1 tablespoon lard
1 medium onion, peeled, chopped
1 clove garlic, crushed
½ cup slivered green pepper
1 16-ounce can tomatoes, drained (reserve liquid)
Salt and pepper

Wipe meat with damp paper towel.

Melt lard in large skillet over moderate heat. Add steak; brown well on both sides. Remove from pan; reserve.

Add onion, garlic, and pepper to the pan; cook, stirring, until onion is tender.

Break tomatoes into small pieces with fork. Add to skillet with ½ cup reserved tomato liquid; mix well. Season with salt and pepper. Add steaks; bring to boil. Cover; reduce heat to low. Cook 1¼ hours or until meat is fork-tender.

Serve steak topped with sauce, accompanied by noodles or potatoes. Makes 4 servings.

stuffed kohlrabi

liver goulash

1 pound liver (beef, calves, or pork), unsliced
3 tablespoons lard or bacon fat
2 medium onions, peeled, sliced
1 green pepper, cleaned, cut into strips
3 tablespoons flour
Salt and pepper
2 tablespoons tomato paste
1½ cups hot beef broth
1 teaspoon crumbled dried marjoram

Put liver in freezer 10 minutes or until ice crystals start to form. Remove from freezer; cut into 1-inch cubes. Place in colander to drain for few minutes.

Heat lard in heavy skillet. Add onions; cook over moderate heat until lightly browned. Remove from pan with slotted spoon.

Add green pepper to pan; sauté until crisp-tender. Remove; reserve.

Combine flour, salt, and pepper; mix well.

Dredge liver in flour mixture, coating well. Reserve excess flour. Add liver to hot fat; cook, stirring, until browned.

Dissolve tomato paste in hot broth; pour over liver. Add onions, green pepper, and marjoram; cover. Cook over low heat 10 minutes.

Combine 1 tablespoon reserved flour mixture with 1 tablespoon water. Stir into liver mixture; cook, stirring, until thickened. Makes 4 servings.

liver goulash

lecsó with meat

¾ pound veal shoulder, cut into 1½-inch cubes
¾ pound pork shoulder, cut into 1½-inch cubes
4 slices bacon, diced
1 large onion, peeled, chopped
1 tablespoon Hungarian sweet paprika
1½ cups beef broth
Salt and pepper
2 tablespoons raw long-grain rice
1 16-ounce can peeled tomatoes, broken up
2 green peppers, seeded, cut into strips

Wipe meat with damp cloth; cut off excess fat.

Cook bacon in large saucepan until crisp. Remove from pan; drain well. Crumble; reserve.

Add meat cubes to pan; brown on all sides. Remove meat.

Add onion to pan; sauté until tender. Remove from heat; stir in paprika. Add beef broth, salt, pepper, and meat cubes; stir well. Bring to boil; cover. Reduce heat to low; cook 1 hour. Add rice, tomatoes, green peppers, and reserved bacon; stir well. Simmer 40 minutes.

Serve with crusty bread and red wine. Makes 4 servings.

lecsó with meat

stuffed breast
of veal

1 3- to 4-pound veal breast with pocket cut next to bone for
   stuffing
8 slices stale bread
Milk
5 tablespoons butter or margarine
1 small onion, finely minced
½ cup chopped mushrooms
1 egg, well-beaten
2 tablespoons chopped parsley
½ teaspoon crumbled dried tarragon
Salt and pepper
1 cup beef broth or stock
½ cup white wine
1 bay leaf

Rinse veal in cold water; pat dry. Set aside.

Cut crusts from bread; save for bread crumbs. Place bread in bowl.
Add small amount of milk; let stand few minutes.

Melt 2 tablespoons butter in small saucepan. Add onion; sauté 2
minutes. Add mushrooms; sauté until tender.

Squeeze liquid from bread. Combine bread, onion, mushrooms,
egg, parsley, and seasonings in mixing bowl; mix well.

Lightly salt pocket in veal breast. Fill with stuffing mixture; skewer
shut. Rub outside of veal with salt and pepper.

Melt 3 tablespoons butter in Dutch oven. Add veal breast; brown
well on all sides. Add broth, wine, and bay leaf; cover. Bake in
350°F oven 2½ hours, basting with pan juices every 30 minutes.
Remove from pan; let stand 15 minutes before slicing. Cut into ½-
inch-thick slices, using very sharp knife. Thicken pan juices and
serve with roast if desired. Makes 6 servings.

rabbit with
onions
and apple

1 2½ to 3-pound rabbit,   1 large tart apple, peeled, cut
   disjointed   into slices
4 slices bacon   1 12-ounce can beer
6 tablespoons flour   ¼ teaspoon crumbled dried thyme
Salt and pepper   1 teaspoon sugar
1 large onion, peeled, sliced   2 tablespoons water

Wash rabbit; pat dry.

Cook bacon in Dutch oven until crisp; drain. Crumble; reserve.

Combine 4 tablespoons flour, salt, and pepper; dredge rabbit in
mixture, coating well. Brown in hot bacon drippings. Remove rabbit from the pan.

Add onion to pan; sauté over moderate heat until tender. Add apple, beer, seasonings, and bacon; stir well. Add rabbit; bring to boil
over moderate heat. Cover; reduce heat to low. Cook 1 to 1½
hours or until rabbit is fork-tender. Transfer rabbit to platter; keep
warm.

Combine 2 tablespoons flour and water; mix well. Add to gravy;
cook over low heat, stirring, until thickened.

Serve rabbit with gravy and bread or Potato Dumplings (see Index).
Makes 4 servings.

poultry and eggs

roast stuffed chicken

1 4-pound roasting chicken
6 tablespoons butter
1 cup chopped onion
1 cup sliced mushrooms
7 thin slices white bread, crusts removed, cubed
¼ cup minced fresh parsley
1 egg, lightly beaten
Salt and pepper
2 tablespoons melted butter
½ teaspoon Hungarian sweet paprika
1 tablespoon dry sherry

Wash chicken; pat dry. Remove liver from giblet pack. Wash well; set aside. Reserve remaining giblets for another use.

Melt 6 tablespoons butter in heavy skillet. Add onion and liver; sauté 3 minutes. Add mushrooms; cook, stirring, until liver is well-browned and onion transparent. Remove pan from heat. Finely chop chicken liver.

Combine bread cubes, onion, mushrooms, butter, liver, parsley, egg, salt, and pepper in mixing bowl; mix well. Stuff chicken with mixture; truss. Secure neck opening with skewer.

Combine 2 tablespoons melted butter, paprika, sherry, salt, and pepper; mix well.

Place chicken in roasting pan; brush well with butter mixture. Roast at 350°F 1¼ to 1½ hours or until juices run clear when breast is pierced with sharp knife. Baste several times with butter mixture while cooking.

Remove stuffing, carve chicken, and serve. Thicken pan juices for gravy if desired. Makes 4 to 5 servings.

fried chicken

1 2½- to 3-pound frying chicken, cut up
⅓ cup flour
½ teaspoon salt
¼ teaspoon pepper
2 eggs
2 tablespoons milk
1 cup fine dry bread crumbs
1 tablespoon parsley flakes
1 teaspoon Hungarian sweet paprika
Oil or shortening for frying

Wash chicken; pat dry.

Combine flour, salt, and pepper in paper bag. Add chicken, few pieces at a time; shake to coat with flour mixture.

Beat eggs and milk together in shallow bowl.

Combine bread crumbs, parsley, and paprika.

Dip chicken pieces first in egg mixture, then in crumbs, coating well.

Heat 1½ inches oil in heavy skillet over moderate heat. Fry chicken until golden, turning once. Drain on absorbent paper. Place on baking sheet; bake in 350°F oven 15 to 20 minutes or until juices run clear when chicken is pierced with knife. Makes 4 servings.

chicken paprikas

1 3-pound frying chicken, cut up
½ cup flour
Salt and pepper
4 tablespoons butter or margarine
1 medium onion, peeled, sliced
½ pound mushrooms, sliced
1 tablespoon Hungarian sweet paprika
1 cup chicken broth
½ cup dry white wine
2 tablespoons flour
½ cup sour cream

Wash chicken well; pat dry.

Combine flour, salt, and pepper in plastic bag. Add chicken pieces a few at a time; shake to coat.

Melt butter in Dutch oven or kettle over moderate heat. Add chicken; brown well on all sides. Remove from pan.

Add onion to kettle; cook until lightly browned. Remove from pan with slotted spoon; reserve.

Add mushrooms to pan; cook until tender. Remove pan from heat; add paprika. Stir in chicken broth and wine; add onion and chicken. Return to heat. Bring mixture to boil over moderate heat; cover. Reduce heat to low; cook 50 to 60 minutes or until chicken is tender.

Combine flour and sour cream; stir well.

Remove chicken from pan; keep warm.

Stir sour-cream mixture into pan juices; cook over very low heat until thickened.

Pour sauce over chicken. Serve with rice, noodles, or dumplings. Makes 4 servings.

chicken livers paprikash

1 pound chicken livers
4 tablespoons butter or margarine
1 cup thinly sliced onions
1 clove garlic, peeled, mashed
1 tablespoon Hungarian sweet paprika
Salt and pepper
1 cup chicken broth
¼ cup sour cream
1 tablespoon flour

Rinse livers; drain very well. Remove fat or connective tissue.

Melt butter in large heavy skillet over moderate heat. Add onions and garlic; cook, stirring, until browned. Remove from heat. Add paprika, salt, and pepper; stir well. Add chicken broth; cover. Bring to boil. Reduce heat to low; cook 15 to 20 minutes or until livers are done to taste.

Combine sour cream and flour; stir well. Add slowly to liver mixture, stirring well. Cook over very low heat until thickened.

Serve livers with buttered Noodles (see Index) or dumplings; garnish with chopped parsley. Makes 4 servings.

roast turkey with chestnut dressing

1 10- to 12-pound turkey, thawed if frozen

chestnut dressing
¼ cup butter or margarine
1 large onion, peeled, chopped
2 stalks celery, chopped
¼ pound ground veal
¼ pound ground pork
1 turkey liver, chopped
¾ teaspoon salt
Freshly ground black pepper
½ teaspoon Hungarian sweet paprika
6 cups soft bread cubes
¼ cup chopped parsley
1 pound chestnuts, roasted, skinned, chopped
1 egg, well-beaten

5 slices bacon

Wash turkey well; drain. Remove giblet pack; save liver for dressing. Lightly salt cavity of turkey; set aside while preparing dressing.

Melt butter or margarine in large skillet. Add onion and celery; sauté until tender. Using slotted spoon, transfer to large mixing bowl.

Add veal, pork, and liver to skillet; sauté until lightly browned. Season with salt, pepper, and paprika; add to celery and onion mixture. Add remaining stuffing ingredients; mix well.

Stuff turkey with mixture; truss. Place in roasting pan, breast-side-up. Lay bacon strips in single layer over turkey. Roast at 325°F approximately 4 hours or to an internal temperature of 185°F. Allow to stand, tented with aluminum foil, 20 minutes before carving.

Make your favorite gravy with pan drippings. Makes 6 to 8 servings.

roast goose with apple–sausage stuffing

¾ pound sausage, hot or mild
5 tablespoons butter
1 medium onion, chopped
2 stalks celery, chopped
5 cups toasted white bread cubes
1 large apple, peeled, chopped
½ teaspoon crumbled dried marjoram
3 teaspoons salt
½ teaspoon pepper
1 8-pound goose
1 lemon

giblet stock
Goose giblets and liver (including neck if available)
4 cups water
2 celery tops
1 small onion
2 cloves
Salt and pepper

gravy

6 tablespoons rendered goose fat or drippings	Salt and pepper
6 tablespoons flour	1 teaspoon brown-gravy seasoning
	4 cups giblet stock

Fry sausage in heavy skillet until well-browned, breaking into bite-size pieces as it cooks. Drain well; reserve.

Melt butter in skillet. Add onion and celery; cook until tender.

Combine sausage, onion, celery, butter, bread cubes, apple, marjoram, 1 teaspoon salt, and pepper in mixing bowl; mix well. Set aside.

Remove giblet pack from goose; set aside. Remove and discard loose fat in body cavity; reserve for rendering, or discard. Wash goose well; pat dry.

Squeeze lemon. Rub goose inside and out with the lemon juice and 2 teaspoons salt. Stuff neck cavity loosely; skewer shut. Spoon remaining stuffing into body cavity; truss. Be sure to tie wings and legs closely to bird. Place goose on rack, breast-side-up; prick well on breast and thighs so that fat will drain. Roast at 325°F 3 to 3½ hours or until meat thermometer registers 185°F when inserted into breast.

While goose cooks, prepare broth. Combine giblets, water, celery, onion, and seasonings in small saucepan; bring to boil. Cover; simmer 30 minutes. Remove liver; cook 30 minutes. Strain broth; cool. Chop liver and giblets; reserve.

Remove goose to platter when done; tent with aluminum foil while making gravy.

Combine goose drippings and flour in medium saucepan; cook over low heat, stirring constantly, until lightly browned. Add salt, pepper, and gravy seasoning. Slowly stir in giblet stock; cook, stirring constantly, over low heat until thickened. Add reserved giblets; heat through.

Carve goose; spoon dressing into serving dish. Serve with gravy and red cabbage or sauerkraut and applesauce. Makes 6 servings.

duck with cherry sauce

1 5- to 6-pound domestic duckling
1 medium onion, peeled, quartered, studded with 2 cloves
2 stalks celery, cut into thirds

cherry sauce
1 16-ounce can bing cherries or sweet black cherries
½ cup reserved juice from cherries
½ cup Tokay wine
2 tablespoons cornstarch
2 tablespoons cherry brandy

Wash duckling; pat dry. Stuff body cavity with onion and celery. Place duckling on rack in roasting pan. Preheat oven to 450°F. Place roasting pan in oven; immediately reduce temperature to 350°F. Bake 1¾ to 2 hours or until juices run clear when breast is pierced with knife.

Meanwhile prepare Cherry Sauce. Drain cherries well; reserve ½ cup cherry juice. Heat cherry juice to boiling in small saucepan. Thoroughly mix wine and cornstarch. Stir into cherry juice; cook, stirring constantly, until thickened. Add cherries and brandy; heat through.

Discard vegetables from duck cavity. Carve duck; top with Cherry Sauce. Makes 4 servings.

roast goose with apple–sausage stuffing

grilled paprika chicken

3 tablespoons lemon juice
3 tablespoons melted butter
1 clove garlic, crushed
1 teaspoon salt

1 teaspoon Hungarian sweet
  paprika
Freshly ground pepper
1 3-pound broiler-fryer, cut up

sauce

3 tablespoons butter or margarine
1 small onion, peeled, diced
¼ cup chopped green pepper
¼ cup chopped mushrooms
1½ tablespoons flour

2 teaspoons Hungarian sweet
  paprika
1 cup chicken broth
½ cup tomato sauce
2 tablespoons dry sherry

Combine lemon juice, butter, garlic, salt, paprika, and pepper in glass mixing bowl or heavy-duty plastic bag; mix well.

Wash chicken; pat dry. Add to marinade; turn to coat with marinade. Cover or tie plastic bag shut; marinate overnight in refrigerator.

Drain chicken; reserve marinade. Arrange chicken on broiler pan, skin-side-down. Broil 6 inches from heat source, basting occasionally with marinade. Turn; cook 15 minutes, basting twice.

Meanwhile make sauce. Melt butter in medium saucepan. Add onion; cook until tender. Add green pepper and mushrooms; sauté until tender. Add flour; stir well. Cook until bubbly. Remove from heat; stir in paprika; return to heat. Add chicken broth and tomato sauce; cook, stirring constantly, until thickened. Add sherry; stir well.

Serve chicken accompanied by sauce, rice, and green salad. Makes 4 servings.

grilled paprika chicken

scrambled eggs and cauliflower

1 small head cauliflower, trimmed, separated into florets
Boiling salted water
¼ cup butter
1 medium onion, peeled, chopped
4 eggs, lightly beaten
Salt and pepper
Chopped parsley

Cook cauliflower in boiling salted water to barely cover until tender. Drain well; reserve.

Heat butter in heavy skillet until melted. Add onion; cook until lightly browned. Add cauliflower; heat gently 1 minute.

Combine eggs and salt and pepper to taste; pour over cauliflower in skillet. Cook, stirring occasionally, until eggs are set.

Garnish with chopped parsley. Makes 3 servings.

eggs farmer's-style

4 slices bacon, diced
¼ cup finely minced onion
1½ cups cooked fine egg noodles
4 eggs
¼ cup milk
Salt and pepper
3 tablespoons butter or margarine
Chopped parsley

Cook bacon in small frying pan until crisp. Remove with slotted spoon; reserve.

Add onion to skillet; cook until tender. Remove with slotted spoon.

Combine noodles and onion in mixing bowl; mix lightly.

Beat eggs, milk, salt, and pepper together; add egg mixture and bacon to noodle mixture; gently mix.

Melt butter in large heavy skillet over moderate heat. When butter is bubbling and hot, add noodle mixture. Reduce heat to low; cook, stirring, until eggs are set.

Place eggs on warm platter; garnish with parsley. Serve with crisp hot toast. Makes 4 servings.

egg fritters with tomato sauce

6 hard-boiled eggs
1 raw egg, well-beaten
1 cup fine dry bread crumbs

tomato sauce
1 tablespoon butter or margarine
2 tablespoons minced onion
1 8-ounce can tomato sauce
2 tablespoons dry white wine
1 tablespoon chopped parsley

Oil for deep-frying

Peel eggs; pat dry with paper towel. Dip hard-boiled eggs, 1 at a time, in beaten egg, then in crumbs. Coat thoroughly; shake off excess. Chill while making sauce.

Heat butter in small saucepan. Add onion; sauté until limp. Add remaining sauce ingredients; simmer 15 minutes. Keep warm.

Heat 3 inches oil in deep heavy saucepan or French fryer to 350°F. Fry eggs 2 at a time 1 to 2 minutes or until golden. Remove; drain on absorbent paper.

Serve fritters topped with sauce. Makes 3 to 4 servings.

sausage omelet

Excellent

*(combine two...
...recipes).*

2 slices bacon, diced
1 small onion, peeled, sliced
¼ of large green pepper, cleaned, cut into strips
¼ of large red pepper, cleaned, cut into strips (all green pepper can be used if red pepper is unavailable)
¾ cup Hungarian sausage, sliced (or substitute linginica, Kielbasi, or any spicy smoked sausage)
3 eggs
1 tablespoon milk
Salt and pepper
2 tablespoons butter or margarine

sausage omelet

Fry diced bacon in small heavy skillet until crisp. Remove with slotted spoon; reserve.

Add onion, peppers, and sausage to skillet; cook until onion and sausage are lightly browned. Reduce heat to simmer; cover. Cook while making omelet.

Beat eggs, milk, salt, and pepper together until well-mixed.

Heat butter in 10-inch heavy skillet until foam subsides. Add eggs; cook, lifting edges to let uncooked egg run to bottom of pan. Cook until bottom is lightly browned. Top with sausage mixture; fold. Transfer to warm platter. Makes 2 servings.

Note: In winter, substitute ½ cup frozen mixed green and red peppers; add toward end of cooking time for omelet filling.

green-pepper omelet

1 tablespoon lard
½ cup sliced onion
1 large green pepper, cleaned, cut into strips
2 tomatoes, peeled, chopped
¼ teaspoon Hungarian sweet paprika
Salt and pepper
2 tablespoons butter
6 eggs

Melt lard in small frying pan over moderate heat. Add onion; cook until lightly browned. Add green pepper; sauté 2 minutes. Add tomatoes, paprika, salt, and pepper; cook over low heat 15 minutes or until mixture is thick. Keep warm while preparing omelets.

Melt 1 tablespoon butter in 8-inch skillet or omelet pan.

Beat eggs in bowl until well-mixed. Pour half of egg mixture into pan; tilt pan to cover evenly. Cook without stirring, lifting cooked edges of omelet to let uncooked egg run under, until set. Top with half of pepper and onion mixture; fold omelet in half. Turn out onto heated platter; keep warm. Continue in same manner with remaining egg mixture.

Serve omelets immediately, garnished with parsley and accompanied by fried potatoes. Makes 2 to 4 servings.

39

vegetables and salads

lecsó

This delightful combination of peppers, onions, and tomatoes may be served with any plain meat dish or used as a sauce for meat or egg dishes.

2 tablespoons lard
1 medium onion, peeled, sliced, separated into rings
1 pound green peppers, cleaned, sliced
¾ pound tomatoes, peeled, quartered
½ teaspoon sugar
2 teaspoons Hungarian sweet paprika
Dash of cayenne pepper
Salt and pepper

Melt lard in heavy skillet. Add onion; cook over moderate heat until onion is wilted. Add green peppers; cook until crisp-tender. Add remaining ingredients; cook, covered, over low heat 10 minutes, stirring occasionally. Taste for seasoning.

Serve lecsó in vegetable dishes. Makes 4 to 6 servings.

variations
1 pound smoked sausage, sliced, can be cooked in lecsó for an interesting lunch dish.

For a delicious brunch, try adding 4 eggs to lecsó; cook until set. Serve on buttered toast.

red cabbage and apples

1 small head red cabbage
(1 to 1¼ pounds)
3 slices bacon, chopped
½ cup slivered onion
1 tart apple, peeled, cored, sliced

2 tablespoons apple-cider vinegar
1 tablespoon brown sugar
1 bay leaf
Salt and pepper

Wash, core, and shred cabbage.
Sauté bacon in large saucepan until lightly browned. Add onion; sauté until tender. Add cabbage, apple, vinegar, brown sugar, bay leaf, salt, and pepper; stir well. Cover; bring to boil over moderate heat. Reduce heat to low; cook 45 minutes. Remove bay leaf. Makes 4 servings.

mushrooms and sour cream

4 tablespoons butter or margarine
1 small onion, peeled, minced
1 pound fresh mushrooms,
washed, trimmed, sliced
¼ inch thick

½ teaspoon garlic salt
⅛ teaspoon pepper
½ teaspoon paprika
½ cup thick dairy sour cream

Melt butter in large heavy skillet. Add onion; cook over moderate heat 3 minutes. Add mushrooms; cook quickly over moderate heat, stirring occasionally, until tender. Stir in garlic salt, pepper, and paprika; mix well. Remove from heat. Slowly stir in sour cream. Return to heat; very gently heat through. Makes 4 servings.

paprika potatoes

1½ tablespoons lard
¾ cup sliced onion
¾ cup chopped green pepper
1 clove garlic, peeled, minced
4 medium potatoes, peeled, diced

½ cup chopped peeled canned
tomatoes
¾ teaspoon Hungarian sweet
paprika
Salt and pepper

Heat lard in heavy saucepan. Add onion; cook 3 minutes. Add green pepper and garlic; cook, stirring occasionally, until onion is tender. Add potatoes; stir well. Cover; cook over low heat 25 minutes or until potatoes are fork-tender, shaking pan occasionally. Add tomatoes, paprika, salt, and pepper; stir gently. Cook 5 minutes, uncovered.
Serve potatoes hot. Makes 4 servings.

zucchini with dill sauce

4 cups sliced zucchini squash
Boiling salted water
1 teaspoon dried dillweed
1 1.25-ounce package sour-cream-sauce mix
½ cup cold milk
2 teaspoons lemon juice

Cook zucchini in medium saucepan with ½ teaspoon dillweed in boiling salted water just to cover. Cook only until crisp-tender; drain well. Return to saucepan; keep warm.
Combine sour-cream-sauce mix and milk in small mixing bowl; beat 1 to 1½ minutes or until well-blended. Let stand 10 minutes. Stir in lemon juice and ½ teaspoon dillweed; pour over zucchini. Heat very gently 3 to 4 minutes or until heated through. Makes 4 servings.

crisp-fried cauliflower with sour-cream sauce

1 medium head cauliflower (approximately 1½ pounds)
Boiling salted water
2 eggs
2 tablespoons milk
¾ cup dry bread crumbs
2 tablespoons grated Parmesan cheese
Oil for deep frying

Clean cauliflower; wash well. Separate into florets. Cook in large saucepan of boiling salted water until crisp-tender (12 to 15 minutes). Drain well; pat dry on paper towels.

Beat eggs and milk together in shallow bowl.

Combine bread crumbs and cheese on sheet of waxed paper; mix well.

Dip cauliflower in egg mixture, then in crumbs, coating well.

Heat several inches oil in deep-fat fryer or heavy kettle to 365°F. Cook cauliflower, few pieces at a time, in hot fat until golden. Remove with slotted spoon; drain on absorbent paper. Keep hot while cooking remaining cauliflower.

sour-cream sauce
1 1.25-ounce package sour-cream-sauce mix
½ cup milk
1 tablespoon chopped parsley
½ teaspoon lemon juice
½ teaspoon Hungarian sweet paprika
¼ teaspoon Worcestershire sauce
Salt and pepper

Combine sauce ingredients in small saucepan; mix well. Cook over very low heat, stirring constantly, until heated through. Serve over cauliflower. Makes 4 servings.

creamed spinach

½ cup water
¼ teaspoon salt
1 10-ounce package frozen chopped spinach
2 tablespoons butter or margarine
2 tablespoons flour
⅛ teaspoon garlic salt
White pepper to taste
¾ cup light cream
⅛ teaspoon ground nutmeg

Bring water and salt to boil in medium saucepan. Add spinach; return to full boil, breaking up frozen spinach with fork. Cover; reduce heat to low. Cook 4 minutes. Drain well; keep warm.

Melt butter in small saucepan. Add flour, garlic salt, and pepper; stir well. Cook until bubbly. Add cream, stirring well; cook over low heat until thickened. Season with nutmeg. Combine spinach and sauce; mix thoroughly.

Garnish spinach with hard-boiled egg slices. Makes 4 servings.

green beans with ham

green beans with ham

1 pound fresh green beans
2 cups boiling chicken broth
2 tablespoons butter
2 ounces baked or boiled ham, cut into thin strips
1 small onion, peeled, chopped fine
1 clove garlic, peeled, minced
¾ cup sour cream
2 egg yolks
Salt and pepper
¼ cup chopped parsley

Wash beans; snap off ends. Cut into 1-inch lengths. Add to boiling chicken broth in large saucepan. Cook over low heat approximately 20 to 25 minutes or until tender; drain well.

Meanwhile melt butter in skillet; sauté ham until lightly browned. Remove with slotted spoon; reserve.

Add onion and garlic to skillet; cook until onion is transparent. Add onion and garlic to beans; mix lightly.

Beat sour cream and egg yolks together well. Add yolks, salt, and pepper to beans; cook over very low heat 5 minutes.

Transfer beans to warm serving dish; sprinkle with ham and parsley. Makes 4 to 5 servings.

43

snowy potatoes with ham

5 medium potatoes, peeled, diced
Water
1 teaspoon salt
1 3-ounce package cream cheese
½ cup sour cream
¼ teaspoon garlic salt
White pepper
2 tablespoons chopped chives
2 tablespoons butter or margarine
½ cup diced baked ham
Paprika

Place potatoes in large saucepan; cover with cold water. Add salt; bring to boil. Cover; reduce heat to low. Cook 20 to 25 minutes or until tender; drain well.

Combine potatoes, cream cheese, sour cream, garlic salt, and pepper in mixing bowl; beat with electric mixer until smooth and fluffy. Stir in chives. Place in 1½-quart lightly greased casserole.

Melt butter in small saucepan. Add ham; sauté until lightly browned. Scatter ham over potato casserole; drizzle with butter from saucepan. Sprinkle lightly with paprika. Bake at 350°F 30 minutes or until lightly browned and heated through. Makes 4 servings.

44

hungarian sauerkraut

1 16-ounce can sauerkraut
¾ teaspoon caraway seeds
3 slices diced bacon
1 small onion, peeled, diced
1 cup sliced smoked sausage
  (preferably Debrecziner sausage)

2 teaspoons Hungarian
  sweet paprika
2 sweet gherkin pickles,
  sliced thin
4 tablespoons sour cream

Combine sauerkraut and caraway in small saucepan. Bring to boil; cover. Reduce heat to low; cook 15 minutes.

Meanwhile sauté bacon in heavy skillet until crisp. Remove with slotted spoon.

Add onion and sausage to skillet; cook until lightly browned. Remove from heat; stir in paprika.

Drain sauerkraut; add to skillet. Add bacon and pickles; stir well. Cook over low heat 10 minutes.

Serve sauerkraut topped with sour cream. Makes 4 servings.

hungarian sauerkraut

marinated cabbage salad

1½ cups shredded green cabbage
1½ cups shredded red cabbage
¾ cup slivered green pepper
¾ cup peeled seeded cucumber, sliced thin
¼ cup thinly sliced onion
Salt

4 tablespoons water
2 tablespoons white vinegar
1 tablespoon sugar
½ teaspoon celery seed
Salt and pepper
¼ cup shredded carrots

Place each vegetable (except carrots) in separate small dish; sprinkle with salt. Let stand 1 hour.

Meanwhile combine water, vinegar, sugar, celery seed, salt, and pepper in small saucepan. Bring mixture to boil over moderate heat, stirring constantly. Allow to cool.

Place vegetables in sieve; press to remove excess water. Combine cabbage, green pepper, cucumber, onion, and shredded carrots in small casserole; toss well. Add dressing; stir well. Chill 3 hours, stirring occasionally. Makes 6 servings.

beet and apple salad

1 1-pound can crinkle-cut beets (or plain, sliced beets), drained
1 large tart apple, peeled, diced
2 tablespoons finely minced onion

2 tablespoons oil
2 tablespoons apple-cider vinegar
1½ teaspoons sugar
Salt and pepper

Combine beets, apple, and onion in 1-quart casserole; mix lightly.

Combine oil, vinegar, sugar, salt, and pepper; beat well. Add to salad; mix well. Cover; refrigerate 3 to 4 hours before serving.

Serve salad on beds of lettuce. Makes 4 servings.

beet and apple salad

marinated beef salad

2 cups diced cooked roast beef
1 large red pepper, cleaned, cut into chunks
2 tomatoes, diced
1 small onion, finely minced

dressing
1 clove garlic
½ teaspoon salt
3 tablespoons oil
2 tablespoons wine vinegar
Freshly ground pepper

1 head Boston lettuce
¼ cup chopped parsley

Combine beef, red pepper, tomatoes, and onion in mixing bowl; mix well.

Prepare dressing. Peel garlic clove; mash with salt. Combine garlic, oil, vinegar, and pepper to taste in small bowl. Pour over meat and vegetables; mix well. Refrigerate several hours before serving.

Arrange Boston lettuce on chilled serving plates; top with beef salad. Garnish with parsley. Serve with rye bread and sweet butter. Makes 2 luncheon or 4 appetizer servings.

salami salad

2 tart apples, peeled, diced
2 teaspoons lemon juice
¾ pound salami or other flavorful sausage (fully cooked), cut into thin strips
4 medium tomatoes, diced
2 tablespoons pimiento, drained (cut into strips, if canned whole)
1 fresh green pepper, cleaned, diced

dressing
3 tablespoons mayonnaise
3 tablespoons sour cream
1 teaspoon Hungarian sweet paprika
2 tablespoons finely minced onion
Salt

garnish
2 hard-cooked eggs, peeled, quartered
8 small sardine fillets

Toss apples and lemon juice so that apples are coated and will not turn brown.

Combine salami, apples, tomatoes, pimiento, and pepper in salad bowl; toss lightly. Chill.

Combine dressing ingredients; mix well. Chill several hours.

Garnish salad bowl with hard-cooked egg wedges. Top each hard-cooked egg wedge with rolled sardine fillet. Top with dressing. Makes 4 luncheon servings.

noodles, dumplings, and breads

pinched noodles
(csipetke)

½ cup flour
⅛ teaspoon salt
1 egg, well-beaten
Flour for kneading

Combine flour and salt in small bowl. Make well in center; add egg. Mix to form stiff dough. Turn out onto lightly floured surface; knead 5 minutes. Divide into 3 parts; roll each part with your hands to form long cylinder about as big around as your little finger. Pinch off small pieces; add directly to boiling soup, or cook in boiling salted water until tender (about 5 minutes). When done, noodle should cut easily and not be floury in center. Generally, half of this recipe is sufficient for 1½ quarts soup. Pinch remaining noodles; allow to stand on lightly floured board until dry. Store air-tight for future use. Makes approximately 8 servings or enough for 3 quarts soup (expect a lower yield for *galuska* and rolled soup noodles).

variations
Above dough can be rolled to form thin sheet and allowed to dry 2 hours. It is then broken into irregularly shaped pieces and added to soup.
Dough may also be rolled and cut into standard soup noodles.
To make *galuska,* or Soup Dumplings, decrease flour in preceding recipe to 3 tablespoons. Mix flour, egg, and salt well; drop resulting soft dough by ¼ teaspoons directly into soup. Cook as above.

poppy-seed noodles

4 tablespoons butter
1 recipe Homemade Noodles (see Index)
1 tablespoon poppy seeds

Lightly brown butter in heavy skillet. Toss noodles with butter and poppy seeds. Makes 4 to 5 servings.

noodles with walnuts

1 cup finely chopped walnuts
1/3 cup confectioners' sugar
1 teaspoon grated lemon rind
1 recipe Homemade Noodles (see Index)
3 tablespoons melted butter

Combine walnuts, sugar, and lemon rind; mix well.
Toss noodles with butter. Sprinkle individual servings with nut mixture. Makes 4 to 5 servings.

chicken-flavored rice

chicken stock
3 cups water
1 giblet pack containing chicken gizzards, heart, and liver
1 chicken neck
1 chicken back
1 carrot, peeled, sliced
1 stalk celery, sliced
2 sprigs parsley
1 small onion, studded with 2 cloves
1 teaspoon seasoned salt and pepper mixture
1/4 teaspoon poultry seasoning

Combine all stock ingredients (except liver) in large saucepan; bring to boil. Skim foam from surface; cover. Reduce heat to low; cook 40 minutes. Add liver; cook 20 minutes. Remove liver and giblets; mince; reserve. Strain stock; reserve.

rice
2 tablespoons butter or margarine
2 tablespoons finely chopped onion
1 cup converted rice
2 tablespoons chopped carrot
2 tablespoons chopped parsley
1/2 teaspoon crumbled dried marjoram
Salt and pepper
2 1/2 cups reserved chicken stock

Melt butter in heavy saucepan. Add onion; cook until lightly browned. Add rice; cook, stirring occasionally, 3 minutes. Add remaining ingredients; bring to boil. Reduce heat to low; cook, covered, 20 to 25 minutes. All liquid should be absorbed. Fluff rice with fork; stir in minced giblets. Cover; let stand 10 minutes.
Turn rice into serving dish. Serve with any poultry dish. Makes 4 servings.

homemade noodles

Noodles and dumplings hold a unique place in Hungarian cuisine. They are prepared as sweet and savory dishes and are often served for dessert.

1⅓ cups all-purpose flour
¾ teaspoon salt
2 eggs
2 teaspoons cooking oil
2 teaspoons water

Combine flour and salt in mixing bowl. Make well in center.

Beat eggs, oil, and water together; pour into well. Stir with fork from outside of mixture to center. Add small amount of water if necessary, so that very stiff dough is formed. Turn out onto lightly floured surface; knead until smooth and elastic (about 15 minutes). Let rest, covered, 30 minutes.

Divide dough into 4 equal parts; roll 1 piece at a time, as thin as possible. It should be 1/16th inch thick. Roll up; cut into ½-inch strips. Unroll strips; allow to dry several hours on lightly floured towel.

Bring several quarts salted water to boil in Dutch oven. Add noodles; stir to keep from sticking to bottom of pot. Cook approximately 10 minutes. Test frequently for doneness; noodles should still be firm, not mushy. Drain well. Top with melted butter and serve, or use in other recipes. Makes 4 to 5 servings.

noodles and cabbage

3 tablespoons butter
3 cups finely shredded cabbage
1 teaspoon sugar
Salt and pepper
1 recipe Homemade Noodles (see Index)

Melt butter in heavy skillet. Add cabbage, sugar, salt, and pepper; cook, stirring constantly, over moderate heat until lightly browned. Combine with drained noodles. Makes 4 to 5 servings.

noodles with cheese and bacon

6 ounces broad egg noodles
Boiling salted water
3 slices bacon, diced
2 tablespoons finely minced onion
½ cup creamed cottage cheese or farmer cheese
¼ cup sour cream
Salt and pepper

Cook noodles in boiling salted water in large saucepan according to package directions; drain well.

Meanwhile cook bacon until lightly browned. Add onion; cook until bacon is crisp. Remove bacon and onion with slotted spoon; reserve.

Add noodles to bacon fat; mix well. Pour back into saucepan.

Combine cheese, sour cream, salt, and pepper; mix well. Add cheese mixture, bacon, and onion to noodles. Toss to combine thoroughly. Makes 4 servings.

homemade noodles

sweet pancakes
palatschinken

pancake batter
2 large eggs, separated
1 cup milk
½ cup flour
1 tablespoon sugar
1 tablespoon rum (optional)
⅛ teaspoon salt
2 tablespoons melted butter
Butter or margarine for greasing
¾ to 1 cup apricot jam or
   preserves
½ cup ground hazelnuts
2 tablespoons powdered sugar

Beat egg yolks in medium-size mixing bowl until well-mixed. Add milk, flour, sugar, rum, and salt; beat with wire whisk until smooth. Blend in melted butter. Refrigerate batter 1 hour.

Beat egg whites until stiff but not dry; fold into batter, combine well.

Lightly grease 8-inch heavy skillet or omelet pan with butter. Place over moderate heat until few drops of water sprinkled in skillet dance.

Stir batter.

Remove pan from heat; pour in 3 tablespoons batter. Quickly tilt pan in all directions to coat bottom with batter. Return to heat;

sweet pancakes

cook until lightly browned. Turn; cook few seconds on other side. Transfer to warm plate. Continue in same manner, stirring batter before making each pancake. Stack with waxed paper between; keep warm until all pancakes are cooked.

Place 1½ tablespoons jam in center of each pancake; roll. Place side by side on ovenproof platter.

Combine hazelnuts and sugar; sprinkle over pancakes. Heat in 325°F oven 10 minutes.

Serve pancakes with coffee. Makes 10 to 12 pancakes (approximately 6 servings).

potato dumplings

This dough must be handled very quickly, so do not prepare until ready to cook the dumplings.

2 tablespoons butter or margarine
1 tablespoon finely minced onion
2 slices stale white bread
1 6½-ounce package instant
   mashed-potato flakes
   (5 ½-cup
   servings size)
¾ cup water
¼ cup milk
½ teaspoon salt
¼ cup flour
2 eggs, well-beaten
Boiling salted water
1 tablespoon melted butter
2½ tablespoons dry bread crumbs

Melt 2 tablespoons butter in small skillet. Add onion; cook until lightly browned. Remove with slotted spoon; reserve.

Cut crusts from bread; cut bread into small cubes. Add to skillet; brown on all sides. Remove from skillet; set aside.

Place potato flakes in medium mixing bowl.

Bring ¾ cup water to boil. Pour over potato flakes. Add milk and salt; let stand 3 minutes. Mix well. Add onion, flour, and eggs; mix well. Form mixture into small balls 2 to 3 inches in diameter. Force 2 to 3 bread cubes into center of each ball. Drop into large saucepan of boiling salted water; cook 5 minutes. Remove with slotted spoon; place in warm serving dish.

Combine melted butter and dry bread crumbs; sprinkle over dumplings. Makes 10 to 12 dumplings.

savory pancakes
palatschinken

2 large eggs
½ cup milk
½ cup club soda
½ cup flour

⅛ teaspoon salt
2 tablespoons melted butter or margarine
Butter or margarine for greasing skillet

Beat eggs well in mixing bowl. Add milk and club soda and flour and salt alternately, mixing well after each addition. Stir in butter. Refrigerate batter at least 1 hour.

Lightly grease 8-inch heavy skillet; heat until few drops of water sprinkled in pan dance.

Stir batter.

Remove pan from heat. Pour 3 tablespoons batter into pan; tilt pan back and forth to coat bottom of pan completely with batter.

Return to heat; cook until pancake is lightly browned. Cook on one side only. Continue in same manner, greasing pan occasionally, until all batter is used. Stack pancakes on plate with waxed paper between each.

Pancakes can be tightly wrapped and frozen at this point, but must be defrosted before use. Makes 10 to 12 pancakes.

cabbage filling for *palatschinken*

1 recipe Savory *Palatschinken*

cabbage filling
1 small head cabbage, finely shredded
1 teaspoon salt
4 tablespoons lard
1 teaspoon sugar
1 red pepper, cleaned, cut into thin strips
½ cup hot water
3 slices bacon, diced
1 medium onion, peeled, diced
1 teaspoon caraway seeds
½ cup sour cream
1 tablespoon flour
2 tablespoons melted butter
3 tablespoons grated Parmesan cheese

Prepare pancakes first; keep warm in slow oven while preparing filling.

Combine cabbage and salt; let stand 20 minutes. Drain well.

Heat lard in large heavy saucepan. Add sugar; cook, stirring constantly, until golden. Add cabbage and pepper; sauté 10 minutes, stirring constantly. Add water; cover. Simmer 20 minutes.

Meanwhile fry bacon in small skillet until crisp. Drain; reserve.

Add onion to skillet; sauté until tender.

Stir bacon, onion, and caraway seeds into cabbage mixture.

Mix sour cream and flour together; stir into cabbage mixture. Cook over very low heat until slightly thickened. Place some cabbage filling in center of each pancake; roll up. Place on warm platter.

Drizzle with melted butter; sprinkle with cheese. Serve as a side dish with a plain roast or chops. Makes 5 to 6 servings.

ham filling for *palatschinken*

1 recipe *Palatschinken*

ham filling
1½ cups finely minced baked or canned ham
½ cup sour cream
1 egg yolk

Prepare pancakes; keep warm in slow oven while preparing filling.
Combine ham, ½ cup sour cream, and egg yolk in mixing bowl; mix well.

rolled pancakes
2 egg whites, lightly beaten
¾ cup fine dry bread crumbs
3 tablespoons melted butter or margarine

Place 1 heaping tablespoon filling on each pancake. Fold in sides; roll pancake to form small rectangular package.
Lightly beat egg whites.
Dip rolled pancakes in egg whites, then in bread crumbs, coating well. Place on baking sheet. Drizzle with melted butter; bake at 350°F 20 to 25 minutes.
Serve pancakes hot. Makes 10 to 12 stuffed pancakes.

layered pancakes
⅓ cup sour cream
1½ tablespoons light cream
Paprika
Finely minced parsley

Lightly grease 9- or 10-inch pie plate. Place 1 pancake in bottom of dish. Top with 1 heaping tablespoon filling; spread evenly over pancake. Top with another pancake; continue in same manner until all pancakes are used.
Combine sour cream and light cream; pour over pancake stack. Sprinkle lightly with paprika; bake at 400°F 8 to 10 minutes or until heated through.
Cut pancake in wedges. Makes 4 servings.

potato bread with caraway seeds

1 medium potato, peeled, diced
1½ cups water
1 package active dry yeast
2 tablespoons sugar
2 tablespoons shortening

2 eggs
1½ teaspoons salt
2 teaspoons caraway seeds
4 to 4½ cups all-purpose flour

Place potato in small saucepan with water; cover. Bring to boil; reduce heat to low. Cook 10 to 12 minutes or until potato is tender. Drain potato; reserve 1 cup water in which potato was cooked. Steam diced potato a few minutes in saucepan so that it is quite dry; mash without added ingredients.

When potato water has cooled to lukewarm, pour into mixing bowl. Add yeast; stir until dissolved. Add mashed potato, sugar, shortening, eggs, salt, caraway, and 2 cups flour. Beat with electric mixer on low speed 1 minute, scraping bowl frequently. Increase speed to medium; beat 2 minutes. Mix in enough remaining flour to form dough that can be easily handled. Turn out onto floured board; knead until smooth and elastic. Place in greased bowl; cover. Let rise in warm place until double in bulk (1 to 1½ hours).

Punch down dough. Turn out onto floured board; form into round loaf. Place in lightly greased 2-quart round casserole; cover. Let rise until double in bulk.

Bake in 375°F oven 30 to 35 minutes or until loaf is golden and sounds hollow when tapped. Remove from casserole; cool on wire rack. Makes 1 large loaf.

crackling biscuits

½ package active dry yeast
2 tablespoons warm water
  (100 to 105°F)
1¾ cups all-purpose flour
1 teaspoon sugar
½ teaspoon salt
¼ teaspoon pepper

1 egg, well-beaten
½ cup sour cream,
  room temperature
½ cup crumbled crisply fried
  bacon (approximately 8 slices)
1 egg yolk
1 teaspoon warm water

Dissolve yeast in 2 tablespoons warm water. Stir well; set aside.

Combine flour, sugar, salt, and pepper in warm mixing bowl, stirring well.

Combine egg and sour cream. Add to flour mixture along with dissolved yeast; stir to combine. Turn out onto floured board; knead until smooth and satiny. Place in greased bowl; cover. Let rise in warm place 1 to 2 hours or until double in bulk.

Punch down dough; knead in crumbled bacon. Roll on lightly floured surface to rectangle ½ inch thick. Cut into 2-inch rounds. Place on lightly greased cookie sheet; cover. Let rise in warm place 30 minutes.

With sharp knife place several diagonal slits in each biscuit.

Beat egg yolk and 1 teaspoon water together; brush biscuits with mixture. Bake in preheated 350°F oven 20 to 25 minutes or until golden. Makes 12 2-inch biscuits.

desserts

blitz torte

4 eggs, separated
½ cup confectioners' sugar
1 cup granulated sugar
½ cup butter
4 egg yolks
1 teaspoon vanilla extract
1 cup sifted cake flour
1½ teaspoons baking powder
⅛ teaspoon salt
4 tablespoons milk
½ cup chopped pecans
1 tablespoon granulated sugar
1 cup prepared vanilla
    instant pudding

Grease and flour 2 8-inch-round cake pans.

Place egg whites in mixing bowl; beat until foamy. Gradually beat in confectioners' sugar and ½ cup granulated sugar, forming stiff, glossy meringue; set aside.

Cream butter and ½ cup sugar in mixing bowl until light. Add egg yolks and vanilla; beat well.

Stir flour, baking powder, and salt together. Add alternately with milk to creamed mixture; beat well, scraping bowl occasionally. Spread in prepared cake pans. Spread meringue evenly over batter. Sprinkle with nuts and 1 tablespoon sugar. Bake at 350°F 30 to 35 minutes or until meringue is set. Cool in pan.

One hour before serving, carefully remove cakes from pans. Place 1 layer, meringue-side-up, on serving plate. Spread with pudding. Top with remaining layer, meringue-side-up. Chill 1 hour. Makes 8 servings.

gypsy john
rigo jancsi

This dessert is named after a gypsy who
must have had quite a sweet tooth!
Very rich and chocolaty!

chocolate cake
1 cup cake flour
¼ cup unsweetened cocoa
1 teaspoon baking powder
¼ teaspoon salt
3 large eggs
1 cup sugar
⅓ cup water
1 teaspoon vanilla

chocolate filling
10 squares semisweet chocolate
2 cups heavy cream
2 tablespoons rum

chocolate icing
¼ cup light corn syrup
2 tablespoons hot water
2 tablespoons butter
1 6-ounce package semisweet chocolate bits

gypsy john

Sift together flour, cocoa, baking powder, and salt twice; set aside.
Line jelly-roll pan with waxed paper; grease.

Place eggs in small mixing bowl. Beat with electric mixer 5 minutes
or until thick and lemon-colored. Slowly beat in sugar, tablespoon
at a time. Mixture will become very thick. Transfer to large mixing
bowl. Beat in water and vanilla. Slowly add flour mixture; beat until smooth. Pour into prepared pan, spreading evenly to corners.
Bake in preheated 375°F oven 12 to 15 minutes or until cake tests
done. Loosen from pan. Turn out on rack; remove waxed paper.
Invert; cool completely.

Combine chocolate, broken into pieces, and cream in heavy saucepan. Heat slowly, stirring constantly, until chocolate melts.
Transfer to medium-sized mixing bowl. Stir in rum; chill 1 to 2
hours. Beat with electric mixer until stiff and thick.

Cut cake in half crosswise. Place 1 piece of cake on small cookie
sheet. Top with Chocolate Filling; spread to form even layer 1½
inches thick. Top with remaining cake layer. Chill at least 1 hour.

Prepare frosting. Combine corn syrup, water, and butter in small
saucepan. Bring to boil; cook until butter melts. Remove from
heat. Add chocolate bits; stir until chocolate melts. Cool to room
temperature. Spread over top of cake. Chill until frosting sets.

Cut cake into 12 squares; arrange on decorative plate. Makes 12
servings.

strudel

Choose 1 filling recipe:

apple filling
1½ cups peeled, sliced tart apples
¼ cup golden raisins
¼ cup chopped walnuts
¼ cup sugar
¼ teaspoon ground cinnamon
¾ teaspoon grated lemon peel

nut filling
1½ cups ground nuts (walnuts, almonds, pecans, and hazelnuts in any combination you prefer)
½ cup condensed milk
¼ cup golden raisins

cherry filling
1¼ cups well-drained pitted sour cherries, fresh or canned
¾ cup sugar
½ cup fine dry crumbs
¼ cup ground almonds
Dash of ground mace

strudel
4 strudel leaves (approximately 16½ ×12)
4 tablespoons melted sweet butter
2 tablespoons fine dry bread crumbs
1 egg yolk, well-beaten

First make filling. Combine all ingredients for filling of your choice in small bowl; mix well. Set aside.

You will need 2 linen tea towels. Spread 1 on table or counter. Lightly dampen other towel.

Unwrap strudel leaves. Unroll on dampened towel; cover with plastic wrap.

Place 1 strudel leaf on dry tea towel. Brush with butter or sprinkle with ½ tablespoon bread crumbs. Top with another strudel leaf. Continue in this manner until 4 leaves have been used. With long side of rectangular strudel leaves facing you, arrange filling in 3-inch-wide band, 1 inch from edge of dough, leaving 1½ inches free on both ends. Roll up like jelly roll, using towel to support dough. Carefully transfer to lightly greased cookie sheet. Turn ends under to seal. Cut several slits in top of roll. Brush with egg yolk. Bake in preheated 375°F oven 25 minutes or until golden.

Carefully remove strudel from cookie sheet; place on platter. Makes 6 servings.

decker pastry

4 cups flour, unsifted
4 teaspoons baking powder
2 cups sugar
1 cup butter or margarine
4 egg yolks, lightly beaten

1 cup sour cream
1 26-ounce jar cherry pie filling
4 egg whites
1 cup ground walnuts

Thoroughly combine flour, baking powder, and 1 cup sugar in mixing bowl. Cut in butter until mixture resembles coarse crumbs. Add egg yolks and sour cream; mix well to form thick dough. Press evenly in lightly greased 10½ × 15½-inch baking sheet. Be sure to make ½-inch-high rim around edge of crust. Spread with pie filling. Bake at 350°F 25 minutes.

Meanwhile beat egg whites until stiff but not dry. Fold in 1 cup sugar. Spread over pie filling. Sprinkle with walnuts. Return to oven; bake 15 minutes or until lightly browned. Allow to cool; cut into squares. Makes 12 servings.

raspberries with tokay cream

1 pint fresh raspberries (or 1 package frozen raspberries, defrosted)
5 medium egg yolks
6 tablespoons sugar
1 pinch salt
1 tablespoon lemon juice
1 teaspoon grated lemon rind
¾ cup Tokay wine

Wash raspberries (if fresh); drain well. Divide evenly among 4 crystal goblets or sherbet dishes.

Beat egg yolks in top of double boiler until well-mixed. Beat in sugar and salt. Slowly add lemon juice, lemon rind, and wine; beat until foamy. Place over simmering water; beat constantly with wire whip until mixture becomes thick and hot. Pour over raspberries. Makes 4 servings.

kiffels

8 ounces cream cheese
⅔ cup butter
2½ cups sifted flour

nut filling
1 egg white
12 ounces shelled English walnuts, ground
½ cup granulated sugar

Confectioners' sugar

Make sure cream cheese and butter are at room temperature before starting this recipe.

Combine cream cheese, butter, and flour in mixing bowl; work mixture well with your hands until stiff dough is formed. Divide into 60 small pieces; roll into balls. Refrigerate, covered, overnight.

The following day prepare filling before rolling dough. Beat egg white in small mixing bowl until stiff but not dry. Add walnuts and granulated sugar; mix well.

Roll dough to small thin ovals on board dusted with confectioners' sugar. Place rounded ½ teaspoons filling on each oval; roll up. Pinch ends shut; form into crescent shapes. Place on ungreased cookie sheet. Bake in preheated 375°F oven on middle rack approximately 10 minutes or until lightly browned. Remove from oven; cool on rack. Store in airtight container. Makes 5 dozen cookies.

raspberries with tokay cream

hussar's kisses

½ cup butter or margarine
¼ cup sugar
2 egg yolks
2 teaspoons lemon juice
½ teaspoon grated lemon rind
1½ cups all-purpose flour (do not sift)
2 egg whites, lightly beaten
1¼ cups ground or grated blanched almonds (walnuts or other nuts
    may be substituted)
Apricot or plum jam or canned leckvar (poppy-seed) filling

Cream butter and sugar until light. Add egg yolks, lemon juice, and lemon rind; mix well. Thoroughly blend in flour. Refrigerate dough 2 hours.

Using teaspoon of dough for each cookie, form into 1-inch balls. Dip in egg white; roll in nuts. Place 1 inch apart on ungreased cookie sheets. Indent top of each cookie with your thumb to form small hollow. If using leckvar, fill hollows with ½ teaspoon filling before baking. Bake in preheated 375°F oven 10 minutes or until lightly browned. Remove from cookie sheet; if using jam, fill hollows now. Allow to cool on rack. Makes 2½ to 3 dozen cookies.

hussar's kisses

index